# 60 SUPER SIMPLE MORE MAGIC TRICKS

By Shawn McMaster

Illustrated by Leo Abbett

LOWELL HOUSE JUVENILE

LOS ANGELES

NTC/Contemporary Publishing Group

*For my daughter, Peri, whose blue eyes always put me under her spell.*

— *S.M.*

## ACKNOWLEDGMENTS

Thanks go to Max Maven. His knowledge of the history and details of magic amazes me. Eternal thanks to my parents for that "Show Stoppers Showcase" magic set in 1969, and a loving thanks to my wife, Theresa, for her continued support through the good times and the bad.

Published by Lowell House
A division of NTC/Contemporary Publishing Group, Inc.
4255 West Touhy Avenue, Lincolnwood (Chicago), Illinois 60712 U.S.A.

Managing Director and Publisher: Jack Artenstein
Director of Publishing Services: Rena Copperman
Editorial Director: Brenda Pope-Ostrow
Director of Juvenile Development: Amy Downing
Typesetter: Treesha R. Vaux

Lowell House books can be purchased at special discounts when ordered in bulk for premiums and special sales. Please contact Customer Service at the address above, or call 1-800-323-4900.

Printed and bound in the United States of America

Library of Congress Catalog Card Number: 98-75616

ISBN: 0-7373-0155-4

10 9 8 7 6 5 4 3 2

# CONTENTS

1. The Undulating Utensil ...........................4

2. The Disappearing What? ........................5

3. The Disappearing Coin! ..........................6

4. The Object Oracle ..................................7

5. Calling Card ...........................................8

6. You Name It...........................................10

7. The Cry-Baby Quarter ..........................11

8. Water, Water Everywhere . . . ...............12

9. Lie De*deck*tor ......................................14

10. The Peculiar Paper Pieces.....................15

11. The Floating Friend...............................16

12. The Indestructible Handkerchief..........18

13. Cutting a Person in Half .......................20

14. The Haunted Half and Handkerchief ..22

15. *Can* You Do It? ...................................24

16. Where's the Queen? ..............................25

17. The Whirligig Coin ...............................26

18. Balancing Act .......................................27

19. A Mental Picture ..................................28

20. The Standing Pencil ..............................30

21. The Straw and Spud Challenge ............31

22. The Coin and Cloth Caper ....................32

23. Any Color Called....................................33

24. A Stand-Out Card Trick.........................34

25. Snatch the Coin ....................................36

26. Plastic Attraction ..................................37

27. How Many Pieces Do You Have? ..........38

28. The Hole in the Back of My Neck ........40

29. A Tear-able Challenge............................41

30. The Coin Will Tell .................................42

31. It's a Corker!.........................................43

32. The King Freaked Out! .........................44

33. The Spring/Ring Thing .........................46

34. The Mysterious Missing Card................47

35. If at First You Don't Succeed . . . ..........48

36. Baffling Bills .........................................50

37. The Daredevil Ping-Pong Ball...............51

38. Double Your Money...............................52

39. Into Thin Air!.......................................53

40. The Transformation Tube ......................54

41. As Many and Enough Left Over ............56

42. The Silent Talking Cards.......................58

43. A "Free" Choice ....................................60

44. An Impressive Premonition ..................61

45. A Magical Mind-Meld ...........................62

46. The Paper Ring Flight ...........................64

47. The Magic Wish Dish.............................65

48. The Lazy Magician .................................66

49. The Morphing Strings ...........................67

50. Out of the Bag.......................................68

51. The Image of Your Card.........................69

52. A Delicate Balance ................................70

53. The Coffee Cup-Coin Connection..........71

54. The Peek-a-Boo Card .............................72

55. Coin A-Go-Go ........................................74

56. Where Did It Go? ..................................75

57. Boo!......................................................76

58. Seein' Spots! .........................................78

59. The Spooky Singing Goblet ...................79

60. The Rising Card .....................................80

# THE UNDULATING UTENSIL

**1**

*You cause a spoon to magically float in the air.*

## WHAT YOU'LL NEED

• handkerchief, bandana, or cloth napkin • spoon-fork setup

## GETTING READY

**1** Fit the handle of a spoon securely between two tines, or "teeth," of a fork.

**2** With the thumb and forefinger of one hand, hold the spoon/fork setup by the end of the fork's handle, your palm facing toward you. The fork should be positioned horizontally, with the spoon balanced upright between the tines of the fork.

**3** Now hold a handkerchief in front of this setup by clipping one of the two top corners between the index and middle fingers of each hand. The handkerchief should extend toward the floor.

## SHOWTIME!

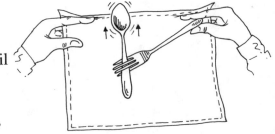

Begin by facing your audience, holding the handkerchief as described. Slowly move your finger and thumb (your right if you're right-handed, left if you're left-handed) upward until half of the bowl, or round part, of the spoon appears above the top of the cloth. Move your fingers back down. Then move them up again, this time letting more of the spoon appear. It will look as if the spoon is floating.

---

**NOTE:** Be careful to keep the fork hidden at all times. Moving the spoon high enough for the fork to appear above the top of the handkerchief will ruin the illusion.

# THE DISAPPEARING WHAT?

*You display a coin and announce to your friends that you will make it vanish with three taps of your magic pencil. One, two, three! The coin is still there, but your pencil has vanished!*

## WHAT YOU'LL NEED
**• coin • pencil, not sharpened**

## SHOWTIME!

**❶** Stand with one side toward your friends (your left side if you're right-handed, right side if you're left-handed). Display the coin in the palm of your hand that's facing outward. Tell your friends the coin will disappear when you tap it three times with the pencil.

**❷** Holding the pencil by one end with the fingers of your other hand, bring the pencil up into the air until it is even with your ear. Then bring the pencil down and tap the coin with it, saying, "One!"

**❸** Bring the pencil up again to exactly the same height and then down again, tapping the coin and saying, "Two!"

**❹** Bring the pencil up once again, but this time quickly slide it behind your ear and leave it there. Without missing a beat, bring your now-empty hand down, saying, "Three!" Look startled that the pencil has vanished; then turn and make your exit, mumbling something about having to practice this trick some more.

---

**NOTE:** You *must not* pause between tap number two and tap number three. All three taps must be done at *exactly* the same beat.

# 3 THE DISAPPEARING COIN!

*Same as "The Disappearing What?" trick on page 5, but this time the coin really vanishes!*

## WHAT YOU'LL NEED
**• table • coin • pencil**

## SHOWTIME!

❶ Begin by being seated at a table—*don't stand.*

❷ The coin should be held in the palm of your hand as in "The Disappearing What?" trick. Proceed exactly as described in "The Disappearing What?" finally leaving the pencil behind your ear. When you reach "Three!" act startled that the pencil has vanished and look at your friends. At first they will seem surprised. But then they will notice the pencil stuck behind your ear and laugh.

❸ Laugh with them and reach up with your free hand to remove the pencil. At the same time, quickly tip your hand holding the coin toward you, dumping the coin in your lap.

❹ Now close that hand into a fist, pretending to still hold the coin inside.

❺ Say, "That was just a joke. Let me *really* make the coin disappear!" Tap your closed fist with the pencil and open your hand to show the coin has vanished.

# THE OBJECT ORACLE

*You correctly identify the one object that everybody in the room was thinking of!*

## WHAT YOU'LL NEED
• secret helper

## GETTING READY

You and a friend who will be your secret helper agree to a color signal that will help you guess the identity of the chosen object.

## SHOWTIME!

❶ Instruct your audience to select and agree on one object, *any* object, in the room once you exit. Leave the room.

❷ Once the audience has decided on an object, you are called back in. Your friend begins walking around the room, touching objects. None of these should be the chosen object. Every time your friend touches something, he or she asks you, "Is this it?" Every time, you answer no.

❸ After a few objects, your friend must touch an object that is the color you two have agreed on. You still say no to this object, but that is your signal—the next object your friend touches will be the chosen object. When he or she touches that object, you, of course, say yes. Everyone will be amazed.

**NOTE:** This trick can be repeated, though not too many times. It is important that your friend touch the chosen object *right after* he or she touches the object that is your signal color. Also, if the object that is chosen by the audience happens to be the same color as your signal color, don't panic. Let's say, for example, that your signal color is red, and the object your audience chooses is red. Your friend just needs to touch another red object before the chosen red object.

# CALLING

# CARD

*Your mysterious friend correctly guesses a card freely selected by a volunteer* over the phone!

## WHAT YOU'LL NEED
• volunteer • deck of cards • telephone
• secret helper in another location (*not at the location of the trick*)

## GETTING READY

You and your friend must memorize the following secret code:
Your friend answers his phone and says, "Hello." You answer, "Yes. May I speak to the Magic Mindreader please?" This is your friend's cue to begin naming card values slowly in order. (Example: "Ace . . . 2 . . . 3 . . . 4 . . . ," etc.) Once your friend names the number of the chosen card, you interrupt him by saying, "Hello, Magic Mindreader?" That tells your friend the number of the selected card. He now begins to slowly name the card suits. (Example: "Clubs . . . diamonds . . . hearts . . . spades."). Once your friend names the suit of the selected card, you interrupt again and say, "Hold on." You are then ready to hand the phone to a volunteer from the audience. Your friend now knows the name of the selected card and can tell the volunteer. (The "Showtime!" instructions provide an example with a selected card.)

# SHOWTIME!

**❶** Choose a volunteer and have her select any card from the deck. Tell her to show everybody in the room the selected card. Let's say it is the 5 of diamonds. Be sure to remember the card.

**❷** Tell your audience that you have a mysterious friend called the Magic Mindreader, who will be able to tell the volunteer the identity of her card.

**❸** Dial your friend's number. The conversation between you and your friend should go something like this:

**Friend:** Hello?

**You:** Yes. May I speak to the Magic Mindreader, please?

**Friend:** Ace . . . 2 . . . 3 . . . 4 . . . 5 . . .

**You:** Hello, Magic Mindreader?

**Friend:** Hearts . . . clubs . . . diamonds . . .

**You:** Hold on.

(You now hand the phone to the volunteer.)

**Volunteer:** Hello?

**Friend:** Your card is the 5 of diamonds.

**NOTE:** Your friend should hang up immediately after naming the selected card to avoid any questions the volunteer may have.

# 6

# YOU
# NAME IT

*You write down names called out by friends and place those names into a bag. You then make a prediction. One of your friends chooses a name from the bag, and it matches your prediction exactly!*

## WHAT YOU'LL NEED
**• about a dozen slips of paper • pencil or pen • bag • table • big piece of paper**

## SHOWTIME!

**1** Ask your friends, one by one, to name a person—living or dead—and you will write the names on slips of paper and put them into the bag on the table.

**2** When the first name is called out, write it down and toss the slip of paper into the bag.

**3** When the second name is called out, write the *first name again* on another slip of paper and toss it into the bag.

**4** Continue writing the *first name* each time another name is called out. Be sure none of your friends can see what you are writing.

**5** Once everyone has called out a name, you will be holding a bag full of slips of paper with the same name. Pick up the big piece of paper and on it write your prediction of what name will be drawn from the bag (the same name you have written on every slip of paper). Fold up the paper with your prediction on it and place it in plain sight.

**6** Shake the bag a few times and have a friend choose a name from it. Have him or her read it out loud, and you will then proudly display your prediction.

# THE CRY-BABY QUARTER

*You cause a quarter to cry real tears.*

## WHAT YOU'LL NEED
• quarter • wet sponge

## GETTING READY

❶ Get a small piece of sponge wet but not *too* wet. Make sure it doesn't drip water before you are ready.

❷ Hold the piece of sponge secretly behind a quarter. (The sponge piece should be small enough to hide completely behind the coin.)

## SHOWTIME!

❶ Hold up the quarter between your thumb and forefinger, keeping the wet sponge hidden with your thumb.

❷ Tell your friends a lot of people don't know that quarters are the most emotional of all the coins. Offer to demonstrate. Look at the quarter and say something like, "You call yourself a coin? I've seen better-looking silver in my dad's hair!"

❸ Squeeze the sponge with your thumb so the water trickles in droplets to the floor. When the sponge is empty, put the coin and sponge in your pocket. If friends want to see the coin, take it back out and hand it to them, leaving the sponge safely hidden in your pocket.

*You cause a cup filled with water to travel magically from one place to another.*

## WHAT YOU'LL NEED

• scissors • two paper bags (lunch bag size) • table
• pitcher of water • two identical paper cups

## GETTING READY

❶ Using a pair of scissors, carefully cut the bottom out of one of two cups and discard.

❷ You should now have one cup with a bottom and one without. Stack both so that the cup without the bottom goes inside the cup with the bottom.

❸ Using a marker, write the word "START" on one bag and "FINISH" on another.

## SHOWTIME!

❶ Place both bags on the table, next to the pitcher of water. The bags should be open, with the words you marked on them facing your audience. Put the stacked cups behind one of the bags.

❷ Show your audience that both bags are empty.

❸ Pick up the stacked cups and show them to the audience. You should pick them up so your fingers are on one side of the "mouths" of the cups and your thumb on the other. That way, you are hiding the double "lips" of the cups. *It is important for your audience to believe that you are holding one cup!* Place the stacked cups into the bag marked "FINISH."

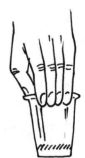

**4** Pick up the pitcher and pour water into the cups until they are three-fourths full.

**5** Now state that you will magically cause the cup of water to travel to the "FINISH" bag. Start to wave your hands over the bag but stop suddenly, noticing your "mistake." "The cup is already in the 'FINISH' bag," you say. "I put it in the wrong bag."

**6** Reach into the bag, grip the mouth of the *no-bottom cup only,* and carefully pull it out of the bag, leaving in the bag the cup with the bottom (which has the water).

**7** Act as if the cup you are holding has water in it, and carefully place it into the "START" bag.

**8** Now wave your hands over both bags. Quickly and dramatically crumple up the "START" bag, along with the cup that is inside. Reach into the "FINISH" bag and proudly display—the cup of water. Pour the water back into the pitcher and take your bow.

# 9

# LIE
# DEDECKTOR

You use a deck of cards as a "lie detector" to determine whether your friend is lying or not.

## WHAT YOU'LL NEED
• **deck of cards • table**

## GETTING READY

Remember the identity of the card on the bottom of your deck. This will be the key to finding the card your friend selects.

## SHOWTIME!

**1** Fan out the deck of cards on the table and ask a friend to choose a card. As your friend looks at the card, close the fan, straighten up the deck, and place it on the table, facedown. Ask your friend to cut the deck into two equal piles.

**2** Instruct your friend to place the selected card onto the pile she just cut from the top, and then place the other half now on top. This places the card you've remembered right on top of your friend's selected card!

**3** Tell your friend that this deck of cards can detect lies. Explain that you will begin turning cards over. You will be asking her each time if you are holding the selected card. Instruct your friend to say no every time, even when the selected card is shown. Tell your friend that you will get a "vibe" of some sort from the cards when she lies about the selected card. You now begin to turn the cards over, one by one, showing each to your friend.

**4** As you go through each card, look for your "key" card (the one you've remembered). Once you see it, you know the *next* card will be your friend's card.

**5** Once you turn over the selected card and your friend says no, yell, "LIAR!" and watch your friend's reaction.

# THE PECULIAR PAPER PIECES

*You begin with two pieces of paper, one attached to each hand. The papers vanish and reappear at will.*

## WHAT YOU'LL NEED
• two small pieces of paper, no bigger than the fingernail of your index finger • table

## GETTING READY
Moisten and affix two pieces of paper to the nails of your index fingers.

## SHOWTIME!

❶ Extend the index and middle fingers of each hand (with the pieces of paper affixed to the nail) on the edge of the table. All other fingers are curled underneath.

❷ Raise one hand in the air. As you do, curl in your index finger and extend your ring finger. Bring the hand down, striking the table edge with these fingers as you say, "One." It will appear as if the paper has vanished.

❸ Repeat the exact same action with your other hand, saying, "Two" as you strike the edge of the table with your fingers. The second piece of paper has disappeared!

❹ Without missing a beat, raise the first hand again in the air. As it goes up, switch your fingers back to the way they were at the beginning. Strike the table and call out, "Three." The paper is back.

❺ Repeat the same action with your other hand, striking the table edge, shouting, "Four." That paper has come back as well!

# THE FLOATING FRIEND

*You cause a friend from the audience to float into the air!*

## WHAT YOU'LL NEED

• secret helper • low elevated platform, long enough for your friend to lie flat (This can be a couch, low sturdy table, or platform you've made out of wood.)
• blanket or cloth, long enough to completely cover your friend and still have inches of fabric beyond the head and feet

## SHOWTIME!

❶ Start by directing your audience's attention to the platform. The blanket should be lying on the floor in front of the platform. Ask for a volunteer.

❷ Using a little acting talent, your secret helper volunteers with everyone else. (*No one* should know that this has been set up beforehand.)

❸ Pick your secret helper to be your volunteer.

❹ Ask your "volunteer" to lie down as straight as possible on the platform.

❺ Standing behind the platform, reach over him to pick the cloth up by its corners. Once you've gripped the corners, straighten your body back up, taking the cloth along with you. This will block your helper from view. Now pull the cloth toward you so it drapes over him.

❻ As you are picking up the cloth and your helper is safely hidden from view, he quickly rolls over onto his stomach and pulls his arms and the leg that is farthest from the audience in and underneath his body. The other leg should remain straight.

**❼** Once this has been done and the cloth has been draped over your secret helper, make some magical gestures with your open hands.

**❽** As you are gesturing, utter a few magic words. This will signal your helper to slowly lift himself by pushing up on his knee and arms. (Your helper should be doing a slow push-up with one leg extended.)

**❾** Once he has remained in place for a few seconds, your helper slowly "floats" back down to the platform.

**❿** You now begin to uncover your helper. To do this, pick up the edge of the cloth on your side of the platform and begin to move it away from you.

**⓫** Just as previously, once the cloth is fully extended—but before your secret helper comes back into view—he flips over again to his back. Once uncovered, your helper can return to a seat.

NOTE: Your friend should always pretend that he is not a secret helper. After the trick, he should act just as surprised as your audience at the fact that he floated. This is a trick that must be practiced a bit before you perform it for anyone. The timing between you and your secret helper is critical. One flaw in the timing, and the trick can be ruined.

# THE
# INDESTRUCTIBLE
# HANDKERCHIEF

*You push a pencil right through the middle of a handkerchief without harming it in any way!*

## WHAT YOU'LL NEED
**• handkerchief • sharpened pencil**

## SHOWTIME!

**❶** Allow the handkerchief and pencil to be examined by a few audience members.

**❷** Once the items have been returned to you, hold up the handkerchief and say, "This may look like a regular handkerchief to you, but it's not. It is made of a magical material that makes it indestructible. Watch!"

**❸** Drape the handkerchief over your fist (your left if you're right-handed, right if you're left-handed). Once the fist is covered, relax and open it slightly. (It should open until your thumb and fingers, still touching, form a circle.)

**❹** The index finger of your other hand now pushes in the center of the handkerchief, making a small well. *At exactly the same time,* under the handkerchief, your fingers and thumb separate just enough to allow the *middle* finger of that other hand to move into the opening just formed, pulling part of the handkerchief in with it. The fingers under the handkerchief then close—around both the index and middle fingers of your other hand.

❺ You should now be positioned with the right index and middle fingers in the center of the handkerchief. The index finger is in a shallow well directly in the center, and your middle finger is right next to it in a well with no bottom, created by the handkerchief being wrapped around it. Remove your fingers, keeping the wells intact. It should look to your friends as if all you did was make a small indentation in the center of the handkerchief with your index finger. They should not know about the well made by the middle finger.

❻ Now pick up the pencil and push it point first into the well with no bottom. Hold the pencil in place for a second with the still-covered hand, and then hit it sharply downward. This will cause the point to come out the other side of the no-bottom well. When done properly, it will really look as if the pencil has torn through the handkerchief's center.

❼ Push the pencil all the way out the other side. Pause a moment, and then shake out the handkerchief to show that there really are *no holes*! The handkerchief truly is "indestructible."

# CUTTING A
# PERSON IN HALF

*OK, OK. It's not a* real *person! Still, you'll impress your audience with your amazing "sawing" abilities!*

## WHAT YOU'LL NEED

• drawing of your "assistant" • crayons • strip of paper, 8½ inches long and 3¼ inches wide • white envelope (business size) with slits in the flap side • scissors

## GETTING READY

❶ With crayons, draw a picture of your "able assistant" on the strip of paper. Use the entire piece of paper. Decorate the address side of a white business-size envelope to make it look like a magical box.

❷ Seal the flap of the envelope. With a pair of scissors, carefully cut about ½ inch off each end of the envelope.

❸ Now carefully cut two 3½-inch-long slits in the flap side of the envelope. The slits should be near the center and about 2 inches apart. (Be sure you don't cut through the side you just colored.) Keep the scissors handy, and you are ready to go.

## SHOWTIME!

❶ Show your "able assistant" to the crowd and begin to slide it, feet first, into one end of the envelope.

❷ As the feet go in, allow them to secretly come out through the first slit. (Be very careful not to expose the fact that they are sticking out the back of the envelope. Keep them perfectly aligned with the envelope.)

**❸** Keep pushing the assistant into the envelope (secretly guiding its feet into the next slit). To your audience, it should just look as if all of the assistant is sliding directly into the envelope.

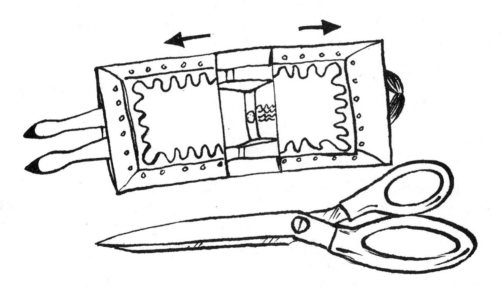

**❹** Holding the envelope horizontally, pick up the scissors and prepare to cut. Position the bottom blade underneath the envelope between it and the section of the assistant that is outside (and between) the slits.

**❺** Cut the envelope through the middle. Separate the two pieces of envelope and show that your assistant is still in one piece! Crumple up the pieces of envelope to get rid of the evidence.

# THE HAUNTED HALF AND HANDKERCHIEF

*You display a half-dollar to your audience. You then cover it with a handkerchief. You make a mystical wave, and the coin has vanished!*

## WHAT YOU'LL NEED
**• two matching patterned handkerchiefs • needle and thread • two half-dollars • table**

## GETTING READY

❶ Have a parent sew two matching patterned handkerchiefs together along the edges. All the edges must be sewn completely closed except for one corner. That corner, along with a 2-inch opening along the hem on either side of the corner, should remain open for now. The person doing the sewing must then stitch down about 2 inches away from one edge of the opening, and then back over to the other edge of the opening. This will create a small 2-inch square pocket in the handkerchief's open corner.

❷ Insert one half-dollar into that corner, and have a parent sew the pocket closed along the hem.

## SHOWTIME!

❶ Place the handkerchief and the second half-dollar on the table.

❷ Pick up the coin and show it to your audience.

❸ Hold it at the fingertips of one hand (your right hand if you're right-handed, left if you're left-handed). Your other hand now picks up the handkerchief by the corner with the coin sewn inside. Begin to drape the handkerchief over the hand holding the coin. Start at the front of the hand and pull the handkerchief back toward you until it is centered over the hand.

**4** As the hand with the handkerchief goes by the hand with the coin, that hand drops the coin it is holding into its palm to quickly grab on to the coin sewn in the corner of the handkerchief. After transferring this corner to the other hand, the hand with the handkerchief continues to move it over that hand until the handkerchief is centered and even on all sides of the hand.

**5** Once it has finished positioning the handkerchief, your hand moves to the center and, from your other hand, grabs hold of the coin sewn in the corner. Your other hand then emerges from the handkerchief, secretly hiding its coin in its palm. It looks, though, as if the hand that positioned the handkerchief is now holding, through the handkerchief, the coin the audience saw at the beginning.

**6** Allow some of your friends to feel the coin through the handkerchief. This will "prove" to them that nothing sneaky has happened. But, while they are feeling this coin, you are sneaking the coin in your other hand into a nearby pocket.

**7** When everyone has had a chance to feel the coin, wave the hand that positioned the handkerchief over the coin, and then, with that hand, slowly pull the handkerchief off your other hand to show the coin has "vanished"!

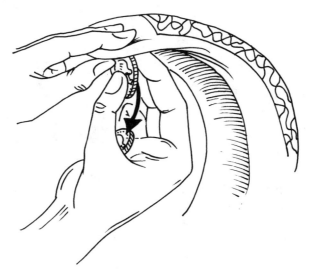

# CAN YOU
## DO IT?

*You challenge a friend to remove a can of soup from the center of a piece of paper without touching the can or knocking the can over. Your friend can't do it, but you can!*

### WHAT YOU'LL NEED

• sheet of paper, 8½ by 11 inches • unopened can of soup • table

### SHOWTIME!

❶ Lay the sheet of paper flat on the table and put the can at its center.

❷ Challenge your friend to remove the can from the paper without touching the can or causing the can to fall over.

❸ Your friend will try and fail.

❹ You now step up to the table and, starting at one end of the sheet of paper, begin to slowly roll the paper, toward the can, into a tube. As the tube reaches the can, keep rolling. The tube will begin moving the can away from you. Keep rolling until the can has moved completely off the other end of the paper and you are left victorious.

# WHERE'S THE QUEEN?

*A strip of five cards is shown to your friends. Four of the cards are black. The other is a red queen. You ask a friend to place a clothespin on the queen. As hard as your friend tries, he is never able to locate the queen.*

## WHAT YOU'LL NEED
• **strip of five cards** • **glue or paste** • **friend** • **clothespin**

## GETTING READY

❶ Arrange the five cards (four black number cards and one red queen) by overlapping them in a long strip and gluing or pasting them in place. The queen should be fourth from the left with only one card overlapping it. Let this strip of cards dry overnight.

## SHOWTIME!

❶ Show your friends the strip of cards so they can see the faces and ask one friend to remember where the queen is.

❷ Hand him the clothespin and turn the strip around so only the backs of the cards can be seen. Ask your friend to clip the clothespin onto the queen.

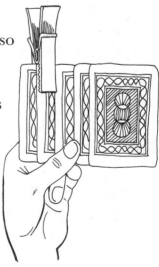

❸ After he has done so, leave the clothespin where it is and turn the strip around. Your friend will see that his guess was *way off*! Most likely, the clothespin will be clipped to the last card. The way the cards are overlapped confuses anybody trying to find the queen. It's sort of an optical illusion. Try it yourself before you try it on your friends. You may end up fooling yourself!

# THE WHIRLIGIG COIN

*A half-dollar begins to spin magically.*

## WHAT YOU'LL NEED
**• half-dollar • table**

## SHOWTIME!

❶ Stand the half-dollar on its edge on the table and hold the coin in place by placing your index finger (your left if you're right-handed, right if you're left-handed) on top of it.

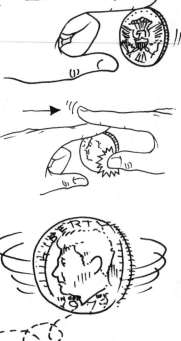

❷ Extend the index finger and thumb of your other hand. Quickly stroke the top of the index finger holding the coin with the extended one.

❸ After a few strokes, allow the tip of your extended thumb to strike the side of the coin. (Because of the quick strokes and because it happens on your side, the audience will not see your thumb hit the coin.)

❹ The coin will begin spinning on the table and will move out from under your index finger.

---

**NOTE:** This trick will take a little practice to get right. If you strike the coin with your thumb too far in, you will end up knocking it over. Practice makes perfect.

# BALANCING ACT

*A cup magically balances on the top of a playing card.*

## WHAT YOU'LL NEED

• **playing card** • **plastic drinking cup (do *not* use glass)**

## SHOWTIME!

**❶** Hold the playing card upright with the face toward the audience. You should be holding the card in your hand (your left if you're right-handed, right if you're left-handed), with your thumb on one long side and your middle, ring, and pinkie fingers together on the other. Your index finger should rest lightly on the back of the card.

**❷** With your other hand, carefully place the cup on top of the card. Allow about three-fourths of the cup to extend past the back of the card. As the cup is put in place, move your index finger from the back of the card up to the bottom of the cup and hold it in place.

**❸** From the front it will seem as if the cup is just sitting there, perfectly balanced, on top of the card.

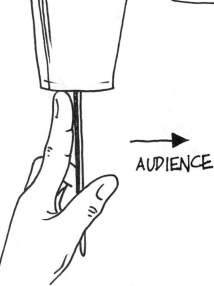

AUDIENCE

# A MENTAL
·····································
# PICTURE

*You correctly predict which picture your friend will select before he or she chooses it.*

## WHAT YOU'LL NEED
• **six index cards, each with a different picture**
• **table • piece of paper • pencil**

## GETTING READY

On each of six index cards, draw a simple picture. The pictures can be anything, but keep them simple.

## SHOWTIME!

❶ Lay the six picture cards out on the table so that your friends can see the pictures. (Let's say that the pictures are of a car, a house, a stick person, a happy face, a tree, and a dog.)

❷ Announce that you will make a prediction of which picture a volunteer will select. On the piece of paper, draw the picture that is on the card fourth from the left. Let's say, for example, that it is the happy face. (No one should see your prediction yet.) Once you are done, fold up the piece of paper and place it in full view of your audience.

❸ Pick a volunteer. Say, "There are six cards here on the table. Pick a number from one to six."

**❹** No matter what number the volunteer selects, you count the cards so that you end up on the happy face *every time*! Here's how:

- If the number selected is one, you say, "OK, we will spell out your number using one card for each letter." Starting at the right-hand side, spell from right to left, "O-N-E," touching one card for each letter you count out. When you are done, you will be touching the happy face.

- If the number two is selected, you count exactly as above, spelling out "T-W-O."

- If your volunteer selects the number three, *count*—do not spell—the cards, starting from the right-hand side.

- If the number selected is four, count the cards, but this time start at the *left-hand side.*

- If the number five is selected, *spell* from the left-hand side.

- If the volunteer selects the number six, spell again from the right-hand side.

**❺** After everyone sees which picture you ended your counting or spelling on, unfold the piece of paper with the prediction and show everybody that you knew which picture would be selected!

---

**NOTE:** Practice the counting and spelling before you show the trick to anyone. That way you will be sure which side of the cards to begin on and whether you need to count or spell when your volunteer calls out the selected number. You *cannot* pause to think when performing the trick. Otherwise, the illusion of naturalness will be lost.

# 20 THE STANDING PENCIL

*You display an ordinary pencil and cause it to stand up by itself!*

## WHAT YOU'LL NEED

• pencil with a pushpin inserted into the eraser end

## SHOWTIME!

❶ Show your audience the pencil: In one hand, hold the pencil by the eraser end with your fingertips. Your fingers hide the pushpin.

❷ Extend your other hand, palm up. Turn your body so that you're facing the audience with the same side as you're holding the pencil. While turning, with your fingers still hiding the pushpin from view, place the eraser end of the pencil at the base of the middle and ring fingers of your other hand. The pushpin goes in between these two fingers and is held in place there.

❸ Slide the hand holding the pencil to the pointed end, and push the point of the pencil gently against the palm of that hand. Now flatten out your hands a bit, keeping the fingers of each hand together. Display the pencil as shown here.

❹ Slowly remove the hand that the audience has seen holding the pencil, and keep your other hand motionless. It will look like the pencil is magically standing upright now on the palm of that second hand.

❺ After the pencil has "stood" there for a few moments, remove it with the first hand. To do this, that hand grips the pencil at the eraser end and takes it from the second hand, hiding the pushpin with its fingers.

❻ Once the pushpin is safely hidden from view, that second hand grips the pencil at the middle and takes it back from the first hand, secretly pulling off the pushpin as it does so.

❼ You can now hand out the pencil to be examined, while the pushpin stays hidden in your hand.

# A N Y   C O L O R

# C A L L E D

*Three crayons are placed in your hands and held behind your back. Your friends call out any one of the crayons, and you successfully bring it out every time!*

## WHAT YOU'LL NEED

• **three different-colored crayons • table**

## GETTING READY

❶ Mark three different-colored crayons in such a way so that you can tell which is which just by *feeling* it. These marks must not be obvious to anybody looking at the crayons.

❷ Let's say your three crayons are colored red, blue, and yellow. With your fingernail, make a small knick in the top edge of the red crayon near the point. Tear back a tiny bit of wrapper on the blue crayon. Knick the edge of the flat bottom of the yellow crayon. (You must remember which mark goes with which crayon.)

## SHOWTIME!

❶ Lay the three crayons out on the table.

❷ Turn your back and put your hands behind you. Allow a volunteer to mix the crayons and place them into your hands.

❸ Turn back around to face your audience. Have the volunteer call out one of the crayons. When the color is named, feel around for the mark that goes with that color.

❹ When you find it, bring that crayon out. Repeat the trick once or twice. You will be correct every time!

**NOTE:** When the color is called out, be dramatic. Act as if you are deep in concentration, as if you are trying to "sense the colors with your mind." *Don't look as if you are feeling around for something on the crayons!*

# A STAND-OUT
# CARD TRICK

*This is an easy way to find a card that your friend selects.*

## WHAT YOU'LL NEED
**• deck of cards • table**

## GETTING READY

❶ You must first set up the deck. Here's how. Separate all the cards into two piles: one pile with all the *red* cards and one pile with all the *black* cards.

❷ Now put one pile on top of the other. You now have a deck of cards separated into two halves: a red half and a black half. You are now ready to begin.

## SHOWTIME!

❶ Select a volunteer.

❷ Pick up the deck of cards and hold it face-down in your palm (your left if you're right-handed, right if you're left-handed). Place the fingers of your other hand on the top of the deck with your thumb at the short end, facing you. Starting at the bottom of the deck, pull your thumb upward, letting the cards flick off it. Look at the faces of the cards as they flash by. Only you should be seeing the faces of the cards. While you are doing this, say to your friends, "I am going to cut this deck into two equal piles."

❸ As soon as you see the color of the faces change, stop and cut the deck there. Place the two halves facedown on the table next to one another. Your audience doesn't know you have separated the deck into two different-colored piles. Look at the two piles and say thoughtfully, "That looks about right."

**4** Pick up one of the piles and spread the cards out facedown in your hands. Ask the volunteer to take any card from that half and to remember the card.

**5** While he is doing this, put down the half you are holding and pick up the other half. Spread this half out just like the first one and tell the volunteer to place his selected card back into this half.

**6** He does this. He has now placed a card of one color into a packet of cards that are all the *opposite* color. His card is the only one that will stand out.

**7** Put both halves back together into one deck. Offer the volunteer a chance to cut the cards. He can cut the cards as many times as he wants.

**8** Now pick up the cards and begin looking through them. What you will see is groups of the same colored cards together throughout the deck. Sooner or later you will come to a single card that is a different color than the group of cards it is with. *This* is the volunteer's selected card.

---

**NOTE:** Make sure the volunteer *cuts* the cards and does not *shuffle* them. If he shuffles them, you are lost. Also, there is a chance that after all the cutting is done, the selected card will end up on the top or bottom of the deck. In that case, you of course will not see the single card inside the deck. You will go through the cards and will notice that there isn't a card "sticking out." Once you notice this, check the top or bottom card. One end will have a different-colored card on it. *That* is the selected card.

# SNATCH
# THE COIN

*You place a coin in the palm of your hand and challenge a friend to snatch it from your palm before you can close your hand. Every time your friend attempts to get the coin, he fails. When you try, with your friend holding the coin, you get it the very first time!*

## WHAT YOU'LL NEED
• quarter

## SHOWTIME!

❶ Place the quarter in your palm. Keep your palm flat.

❷ Ask your friend to try to grab it before you can close your hand. When he tries, close your hand as quickly as you can. Your friend will fail, over and over again. Sometimes, you may even be fast enough to catch his fingers in your hand!

❸ After a few tries, give the coin to your friend. Tell him to lay his palm flat and place the coin on it. Now it's his turn to try and keep you from getting the coin.

❹ Here's how *you* grab the coin. Put your fingers and thumb together as if your hand were in a puppet. Your thumb should not be touching your fingers, however. It should be open and away from your fingers.

❺ Now rotate this hand until the fingers and thumb are pointing down toward the coin in your friend's palm.

❻ Quickly move your hand down, striking the palm of your friend's hand with your fingertips. This causes your friend's hand to be pushed downward a little so that the coin jumps up into your waiting fingers!

# PLASTIC

......................................................

# ATTRACTION

*You "magnetize" the cap of a pen.*

## WHAT YOU'LL NEED
• pen with a cap that is pointed, not flat, at the top

## SHOWTIME!

**1** Tell your friends that you will magnetize the cap of the pen. Hold the pen in your hand (your left if you're right-handed, right if you're left-handed). With the index finger and thumb of your other hand, grip the tip of the pen cap. Rapidly pull the cap on and off the pen, as if you were magnetizing it.

**2** Stop suddenly. Hold the pen horizontally so the point is toward the same direction as your hand gripping the cap. Hold the cap horizontally so it is open in the opposite direction.

**3** Slowly move the pen and cap closer together. As they draw closer to each other, with your index finger and thumb, pinch the cap so it pops out from between your fingers. It will look like the cap was "magnetically attracted" to the pen.

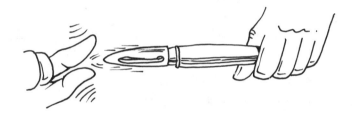

# HOW MANY PIECES DO YOU HAVE?

*Tear a strip of paper into many pieces, and then magically restore it to one sheet!*

## WHAT YOU'LL NEED
• two strips of paper • marker • glue or rubber cement

## GETTING READY

❶ With a marker, write the words "ONE PIECE" on each of two pieces of paper about 20 inches long and 4 inches wide. Try and make the writing on both strips look the same.

❷ Fold one of the strips in half. Then fold it in half again. Keep folding it until you have a square of paper that is about 2 by 3 inches.

❸ With some glue, attach this square to the back of the other strip of paper. You should glue it on or near the end of the strip, on the opposite side of the word "ONE."

## SHOWTIME!

❶ In one hand (your right if you're right-handed, left if you're left-handed) hold your strip of paper by the ends so that the audience sees the words "ONE PIECE." Say to your audience, "I have here one piece of paper."

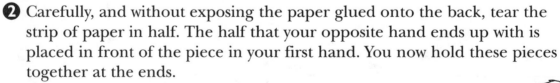

❷ Carefully, and without exposing the paper glued onto the back, tear the strip of paper in half. The half that your opposite hand ends up with is placed in front of the piece in your first hand. You now hold these pieces together at the ends.

❸ Say, "But now it isn't one piece of paper. It's two." Tear these in half, again putting the opposite-hand pieces on top of the others.

**4** Now say, "No matter what the paper says, this is now *four* pieces." Tear them one last time. Again, put the opposite-handed pieces on top of the others. You now say, "And *this* is now *eight* pieces!"

**5** Begin to fold the pieces up together, folding the edges away from you. Make the folds so that they are even with the "secret" paper.

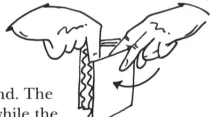

**6** You should now be holding a packet of paper between the fingers and thumb of your first hand. The side facing the audience contains torn pieces, while the side facing *you* is one whole strip.

**7** You now say to your audience, "You know what, though? I really liked it when it was one piece of paper." When you say this, you pass the folded packet over to your opposite hand, turning it around as you do. The whole strip should now be on the side facing the audience. Once the fingers and thumb of the opposite hand are holding the packet, you make a "number one" sign with the index finger of your first hand. This should be timed with you saying the words "one piece of paper."

**8** You now wave your first hand over the packet and, very dramatically, open the strip of paper so the audience can see it is "ONE PIECE" again. Because the torn pieces have been glued back to back with the whole piece, they will stay hidden behind that piece. The torn pieces being folded up together keeps them from separating and falling to the floor.

# THE HOLE IN THE BACK OF MY NECK

**28**

*You prove to your audience that you have a hole in the back of your neck when, without warning, a coin you placed there comes flying out your mouth!*

## WHAT YOU'LL NEED
• half-dollar or quarter (the bigger the coin, the better)

## SHOWTIME!

❶ Tell your friends, "I have a hole in the back of my neck." Look surprised when they say they don't believe you.

❷ Offer to prove it. Show them the coin in your hand (your right if you're right-handed, left if you're left-handed).

❸ Still holding the coin in that hand, reach back behind your head with both hands to "open the hole." As this is being done, be sure that the view of your elbow opposite the hand holding the coin is blocked from the audience by your head.

❹ With that elbow safely hidden from sight, place the coin into the crook of the elbow and bend your arm so the coin stays in place. Do your best to make it look as if you are placing the coin into the back of your neck while you are doing this.

❺ Bring your hands into view with the fingers spread wide open, palms facing the audience. Both arms are bent at the elbows. (The coin is secretly hidden in the crook of one elbow.)

❻ Close the hand of the elbow now holding the coin into a fist, with your thumb pointing up. Open your mouth and place your thumb behind the back of your front teeth.

❼ Quickly flick your thumb off your teeth, moving away from your mouth and straightening your arm as fast as you can. The coin will shoot out of your arm and into the air. It will look as if the coin flew out of your mouth.

# A TEAR-ABLE CHALLENGE

*You give your friend a piece of paper with two tears in it and challenge her to tear the two end pieces away from the middle with only one tear. Your friend can't. You can.*

## WHAT YOU'LL NEED
• **two pieces of paper, 8½ by 11 inches**

## GETTING READY

Make two tears in each of two sheets of paper. This will create three equal strips on each sheet. *Do not* tear the paper all the way.

## SHOWTIME!

**❶** Challenge your friend to tear the two end pieces away from the middle piece in one tear. Your friend will try and only succeed in tearing off one end. She will be left with two pieces still clinging together.

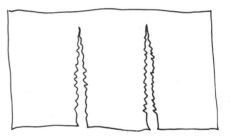

**❷** You pick up the additional sheet of paper and hold both end pieces, one in each hand. Hold the middle piece between your lips. Now pull on the outside pieces, and you will be left with three separate strips of paper. *Ta dah!*

41

# THE COIN
# WILL TELL

*By "listening" to four different coins, you correctly name which one your friend has selected.*

## WHAT YOU'LL NEED
• dime • penny • quarter • nickel • table

## SHOWTIME!

**1** Lay the coins on the table and ask your friend to select one while your back is turned. Tell your friend to hold that coin in his fist and concentrate. Then say, "I will try to read your mind and tell you which coin you select."

**2** As you sit silent for a few moments, pretend you are trying to pick up your friend's "thought waves." What you are actually doing is silently counting to 30.

**3** When you reach 30, tell your friend to put the coin back. "I'm not getting *anything*," you say. You turn around. "Were you concentrating hard?"

**4** No matter what your friend answers here, say, "Let's just ask *the coins* which one you selected." Pick up each coin and hold it up to your ear. Pretend it is talking to you. What you are *really* doing is *feeling* each coin. The one that was held in your friend's fist will be warmer than all the rest.

**5** Once you have held all four coins, you will know by the warmth which one your friend selected. You can now announce the name of the chosen coin.

# IT'S A CORKER!

*You cause two corks to penetrate each other.*

## WHAT YOU'LL NEED
• **two corks of equal size**

## SHOWTIME!

**1** Begin by holding the corks, one in each hand, in the crooks of your thumbs. Both hands are held so the palms are facing you. The corks are upright.

**2** Keeping the corks in place, rotate your hands in opposite directions: One hand (your right if you're right-handed, left if you're left-handed) turns palm down, while the other hand turns palm up.

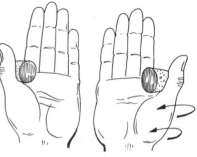

**3** The index finger and thumb of the hand with the palm turned down grip the other hand's cork by placing the index finger on the top of the cork and the thumb on the bottom.

**4** At the same time, the index finger and thumb of the hand, palm up, grip the cork of the hand, palm down. To do this, the thumb must reach under the fingers of the opposite hand to grip what started out as the bottom of that cork. The index finger must reach up from under the thumb of the opposite hand to grip what was initially the top of the cork.

**5** From this position you now separate your hands, taking with them their new corks. As your hands move away from each other, you again rotate them: Your first hand now turns palm up with its cork, and your other hand now turns palm down with its cork. If this moving and rotating is done correctly, you will create the illusion of the two corks passing *right through* each other!

# THE KING
# FREAKED OUT!

*You tell a short story about a king who decided to shave off his mustache with disastrous results!*

## WHAT YOU'LL NEED
**• deck of cards • table**

## GETTING READY

❶ Pull out the king of clubs (a king with a mustache, holding a sword) and the king of hearts (a king with no mustache, holding the sword to his head) from a deck of cards.

❷ Place the king of hearts behind the king of clubs and square the two cards exactly. Hold these cards perfectly straight in your hand (your right if you're right-handed, left if you're left-handed) by placing your fingers on the top end of each card and your thumb on the bottom. The face of the king of clubs should be facing away from you. The rest of your deck should be held facedown in the palm of your other hand.

## SHOWTIME!

❶ Show your audience the king of clubs. (You should be holding cards as already described.) Your audience must believe that you are holding *only one* card. They should not know about the hidden king.

❷ "I'd like to tell you a little story about this king," you begin. "You see his mustache there? He had that mustache for his entire life. Some believe he was *born* with it."

44

**3** You continue your story: "Well, one day he grew tired of the mustache and decided to shave it off." As you are telling this part of the story, you place the two cards facedown as one on top of the deck in your hand. Make sure the cards stay straight. Now place the deck facedown on the table.

**4** "Well," you continue, "he didn't have a razor, so he decided to use his sword. He was very careful and shaved the mustache off completely."

**5** Stop and look around for a second. Then lean in and continue your story in a lower tone of voice. "The king wasn't too stable to begin with," you tell them. "And when he looked in the mirror and saw what he looked like . . . the king *freaked out!*"

**6** As you say that last sentence, turn over the top card of the deck (the king of hearts, which was secretly hidden behind the king of clubs). Point to the sword and say, "He did himself in with his *own sword!*" Your friends will laugh at the story as well as the image of the king "sticking his sword in his head." But they will also be amazed at how the card has *magically changed!*

# THE SPRING/RING THING

*Only you can remove a small ring from a length of spring.*

## WHAT YOU'LL NEED

**• small piece of spring (available in hardware stores)**
**• small metal or plastic ring just big enough to fit over the spring**

## GETTING READY

❶ Slide a small metal or plastic ring onto a piece of spring approximately 2 inches long, its coils not too far apart. Let it hang in the center of the spring.

❷ Now, gripping the bottom of the ring with a finger and your thumb, give it a twist. It is now impossible to slide the ring off the spring without twisting it back to its original position.

❸ Twist the ring back so it is removable. You are now ready to perform this trick.

## SHOWTIME!

❶ Hold the spring by one end so the ring hangs down from the middle.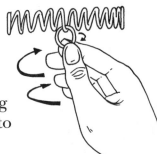

❷ Talk about how easy it is to remove the ring, and then remove it.

❸ Place the ring back on the spring so it hangs as before, and secretly give it the twist. Hand the spring to your friend, and watch the fun as he or she tries to remove it.

**NOTE:** Giving the ring a twist needs very little movement and hardly takes any time at all. You can do it quickly—and secretly—while handing your friend the spring. Practice the twist a few times until you get the hang of it, and see just how quickly it can be done.

# THE MYSTERIOUS MISSING CARD

*Your friend's card mysteriously vanishes from the deck!*

## WHAT YOU'LL NEED
• deck of cards, with piece of double-stick tape on the back of the top card • table

## SHOWTIME!

❶ Fan out the deck of cards between your hands, so all the faces of the cards are facing your friend. (This hides the piece of tape on the back of the top card.)

❷ "Look over all the cards and select one from the middle," you instruct your friend.

❸ After your friend chooses a card, close the deck and hold it in your palm (your left if you're right-handed, right if you're left-handed). The deck should be held upright, still keeping the tape hidden from view.

❹ After your friend is sure of the identity of the card and has shown it to anyone else present, you take it back with your free hand. Be sure to keep the face of the card away from you at all times. Next, place the card square on top of the double-stick tape. To be sure the tape sticks, quickly press the card with your hand as you place it facedown on top of the deck. Don't make this action obvious!

❺ Now place the deck facedown on the table and cut the cards. Snap your fingers, and then turn the deck faceup. Next, spread it out on the table. Because of the two cards sticking together, it will appear as if the selected card has vanished!

> **NOTE:** If you don't want to spread the cards out on the table, you can count them out one by one into a pile. You will only count 51. One card will be missing: *the selected one!*

# IF AT FIRST YOU DON'T SUCCEED. . .

*You try to guess the name of the card your friend is thinking of. When it looks as if you've failed, you suddenly guess it!*

## WHAT YOU'LL NEED
• deck of cards • table

## SHOWTIME!

❶ Deal out three columns of seven cards on the table. You must deal them out faceup from *left to right*. (That is, deal one card faceup, then another one faceup to the right of the first, and a third one faceup to the right of the second. Now start again, dealing the next card onto the first one you dealt, but downward a little so you can see the number of both cards. Repeat on the second card you dealt, and again on the third, until you have seven in each column.) Once you have done this, put the rest of the deck aside. You will not need it.

❷ Ask a friend to think of one of the cards on the table, and you will try to guess which one it is. When your friend says he is thinking of one, you study the cards. Actually, you are only *acting* as if you're studying them.

❸ Tell your friend you can't seem to get it, but to give you another chance. Ask him not to name the card but just to tell you which column it is in.

48

**4** When your friend tells you which column, scoop up each of the three columns and begin stacking them. Pick up the column with the selected card second and stack it on top of the first. The third column is placed on top of the second.

**5** Deal the cards back out, faceup from left to right, *exactly* as before. Act as if you are trying to find the card.

**6** Again, tell your friend you can't seem to get it. Ask which column it is in, and scoop up the cards, putting the column with the selected card in the middle of the stack, exactly as before.

**7** Repeat this whole process one more time: dealing from left to right, asking which column, scooping the columns up with the one containing the selected card going in the middle as you stack them.

**8** At this point, act very frustrated. Pretend the trick is not going the way you planned. Tell your friend you will try it *one more time.*

**9** Begin dealing the cards out again, slowly, just as before. But this time, as you are dealing them out, silently count them to yourself. When you reach the number 11, you will be holding the selected card. Stop suddenly and announce that *this* is your friend's card.

**NOTE:** This trick is mathematical and must be followed *exactly* for it to work properly. Try it a couple of times for yourself before you do it for someone else. If the directions are carefully followed, you will see it works every time.

# BAFFLING BILLS

*A $1 bill and a $5 bill magically change places.*

## WHAT YOU'LL NEED
• **$1 bill** • **$5 bill** • **table** • **pencil**

## SHOWTIME!

❶ Lay the bills out on the table, with the $1 on top of the $5. Both bills must overlap so they form a *V*. The point of the *V* must be pointing at you. The $1 bill must be on your right.

❷ Lay the pencil horizontally on top of the point of the *V.*

❸ Place your hands palm down on the pencil and, with your thumbs, wrap the tip of the *V* around the pencil. Keeping the tip in place, begin to roll the bills around the pencil by rolling the pencil away from you.

❹ As the pencil reaches the ends of the bills, allow the end of the $5 to be wrapped completely around the pencil so it flips out from under the pencil. This secretly switches the bills' positions. *Do not allow the $1 to do this—just the $5.* The fingers of your left hand should hide the view of this action.

❺ Stop rolling at this point, but leave your hands on the pencil to keep everything in place. Ask a friend to put a finger on each end of the bills.

❻ When your friend does as you ask, roll the pencil back toward you. As the bills unroll, she will see the bills have switched positions, even though her fingers were on the bills.

# THE DAREDEVIL PING-PONG BALL

*You magically cause a Ping-Pong ball to balance and roll along a piece of rope.*

## WHAT YOU'LL NEED

• length of rope, 30 to 32 inches long • cotton thread, 30 to 32 inches long
• new, clean Ping-Pong ball

## GETTING READY

Tie the ends of a cotton thread around the ends of a rope the same length, so that the rope and thread create a complete circle. Cut off any excess thread. (The color of the thread should match the color of your clothing. If a match cannot be made, then use black thread and wear dark clothing.)

## SHOWTIME!

❶ Hold one end of the rope in your fingers (your left if you're right-handed, right if you're left-handed). Your thumb should be positioned between the rope and the thread. With your other hand, show your audience the Ping-Pong ball.

❷ Place the ball between your lips, then grab hold of the other end of the rope with your now-free hand. The thumb of that hand should also be positioned between the rope and the thread.

❸ You are now holding a piece of rope between your hands with a thread, tied to each end of the rope, running around the backs of your thumbs. The rope and thread should be kept taut.

❹ Lower the ball down to the rope and place it onto the rope and thread, creating a "track" that the Ping-Pong ball can roll on. You may have to adjust the thread and rope with your fingers.

❺ By tilting one hand up and one hand down, back and forth, the ball rolls from one end of the rope to the other. To your audience, the ball is magically rolling along the rope!

# 38 DOUBLE YOUR MONEY

*You wrap a nickel in a piece of paper. After a magical wave of your hand over the paper, you open it and the nickel has become a dime!*

## WHAT YOU'LL NEED
• two pieces of paper, 5 inches square • glue • nickel • dime

## GETTING READY

❶ Fold a piece of paper into a smaller square in the following manner: Fold about 1½ inches of the right side over to the left. Now fold 1½ inches of the left side over to the right so it is even with the folded edge on the right.

❷ You now have a flat tube of paper. Fold the top down, just past the center. Finally, fold the bottom up so it is even with the top, folded edge. You should now have a small folded square.

❸ Fold a second piece of paper exactly as above. Glue the backs of these papers together. When dry, you should have two folded squares of paper glued together that open on either end.

❹ Fold the dime up in one of the squares. Open up the other square, pick up your nickel, and you are ready to perform the trick.

## SHOWTIME!

❶ Show the piece of paper and the nickel to your audience. Keep the folded-up square with the dime in it out of sight.

❷ Place the nickel into the center of the paper and begin to fold the paper up, covering the nickel.

❸ Wave your free hand over the paper, saying something magical will happen. At the same time, with your other hand, secretly turn the squares of paper over so that the square with the dime is now up facing. Make a magical wave over the paper and open it up to show the dime. You have magically doubled your money!

# INTO THIN
................................................................
# AIR!

*A coin disappears as you toss it to your friend.*

## WHAT YOU'LL NEED
• half-dollar or quarter

## SHOWTIME!

❶ Hold the coin horizontally with your fingers and thumb (your left if you're right-handed, right if you're left-handed). The coin should be held high at the fingertips, and there should be no space between the fingers.

❷ Your other hand moves in to "take" the coin in the following manner: The thumb goes underneath the coin, between the thumb and forefinger of the hand holding it. Above the coin, your fingers begin to curl around the coin.

❸ As soon as the coin is blocked from view by the fingers of the hand "taking" the coin, the thumb of the hand holding it releases enough pressure to allow the coin to slip down to the base of the fingers of that hand. The fingers of your other hand are continuing to curl into a fist—as if it is closing around the coin.

❹ Once that hand has closed into a fist, it moves away from the opposite hand and toward your friend. The opposite hand (still holding the coin) drops to your side slightly open, with the back of the hand facing your friend.

❺ Tell your friend that you are going to toss the coin to him. Make a tossing motion toward your friend with your fisted hand, and at the same time secretly slip the coin into one of your pockets with the opposite hand. Your friend's attention will be focused on trying to see and catch the coin. The coin has "vanished" into thin air!

# THE TRANSFORMATION TUBE

*\* Adult supervision needed to handle scissors.*

*An empty cardboard tube and a handkerchief are shown. The handkerchief is pushed into one end of the tube. A hand is waved over the tube and out rolls a ball! The handkerchief has transformed into a ball.*

## WHAT YOU'LL NEED
**• small handkerchief • hollow plastic ball**
**• cardboard tube, big enough around for the ball to roll through • scissors**

## GETTING READY

**❶** Have an adult cut a hole in a hollow plastic ball, using scissors. The hole should not be too big, but big enough so all of a small handkerchief can be stuffed into it.

**❷** Once the hole has been cut, stick your right thumb through it into the ball.

## SHOWTIME!

**❶** Hold up the handkerchief with your hand (your right if you're left-handed, left if you're right-handed)—keeping the ball on your thumb hidden behind the handkerchief at all times.

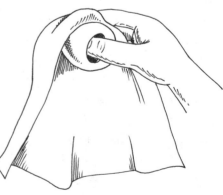

**❷** With your other hand, hold up the tube so your friends can see it is empty.

**❸** Holding the tube upright, begin stuffing the handkerchief into its top. In order to do this properly, you must allow the handkerchief to drape over the front of the tube, blocking the view of it briefly. At the same time, the thumb of your opposite hand sticks the ball into the top of the tube. Your hand holding the tube pushes in slightly on the sides of the tube to hold the ball in place.

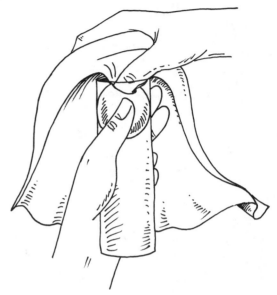

**❹** As you are stuffing the handkerchief into the tube, you are also stuffing it into the hollow ball.

**❺** Once the handkerchief has been pushed completely into the tube (*and* into the ball), wave your now-free hand over the tube and tip it in the direction of your free hand—allowing the ball to roll into that hand.

**❻** As you hold up the ball and show it to your audience, be sure your thumb covers the hole.

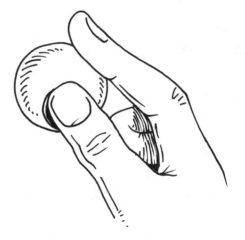

# AS MANY AND ENOUGH LEFT OVER

*This is a version of a trick that was first published over 60 years ago by a magician named Paul Stadelman. It is very simple to do and a real fooler! It has even fooled other magicians!*

## WHAT YOU NEED
• deck of cards • table

## SHOWTIME!

❶ Place the deck of cards on the table and ask a volunteer to remove a small bunch of them. Pay attention as your volunteer cuts off her cards and try to estimate how many cards she took. *Don't worry!* You don't have to be exact—you just need a good, general idea.

❷ You now cut off a bunch of cards yourself. Make sure your bunch contains more cards than the one your volunteer cut off.

❸ Tell your volunteer to count her cards when you turn your back. Tell her to count silently so you cannot hear how many cards she has.

❹ You turn your back, and while your volunteer counts cards, you silently count the cards in *your* bunch. Count quickly, but make sure your count is correct. Remember the number. Let's say, for example, it is 23.

❺ Also quickly, you must now do some simple math. Take your total number of cards (23) and subtract any number from 1 to 5. Let's say it is 3. Silently subtract 3 from 23. You get 20.

❻ Once you turn around, announce to your volunteer: "I will bet you that I have as many as you do, plus 3 extra (the random number you subtracted) and enough left over to make yours equal 20 (the result of your subtraction)."

# AN IMPRESSIVE PREMONITION

*You show your audience a sealed envelope and tell them that there is a playing card inside. A card is selected—and it exactly matches the card sealed in the envelope!*

## WHAT YOU'LL NEED

• **deck of cards** • **envelope** • **card from another deck of cards**

## GETTING READY

❶ Find the card in your deck of cards that matches the single card from another deck.

❷ Once you have found it, put it 10th down from the top of that deck.

❸ Seal the card from the other deck in an envelope.

## SHOWTIME!

❶ Show the envelope and hand it to a volunteer to hold.

❷ Hand the deck to another volunteer and have him select a card as described in "A 'Free' Choice," on page 60. When he is done dealing and has looked at the last card dealt, it will be the one that matches the card in the envelope.

❸ Have the volunteer holding the envelope open it, and let everyone marvel at your "ESP powers"!

# A MAGICAL
# MIND-MELD

*You and a friend succeed in "linking your minds"!*

## WHAT YOU'LL NEED

• deck of cards (with jokers removed) • table

## GETTING READY

Memorize the top card of a deck of cards. (It does not have to be a complete deck of cards, but you must remove the jokers.)

## SHOWTIME!

❶ Suggest an ESP experiment, and spread the cards out facedown on the table. Mentally keep track of the top card (the one you memorized). You must know where it is at all times.

❷ Now tell a volunteer you will call out cards at random, and she is to try and select those cards without looking at the faces. "Take your time," you say. "Wait until it feels right."

❸ The first card you call out should be the name of the card you memorized. Watch your volunteer to see if she selects that card. Chances are good that she will not.

❹ Whichever card she selects, take it from her. Look at it, not letting her see the face. Say, "Not bad," and put it aside, face-down. Call out another card: the card you just looked at.

❺ Your volunteer will select another card and hand it to you. You look at this card and assure the volunteer that she is doing well. You then put the card with the other one.

# THE MAGIC
# WISH DISH

*Three coins are placed on a plate. You wish for five, and you get them!*

## WHAT YOU'LL NEED

**• five coins (two must be a penny and dime) • small paper plate
• paper gum wrapper • clear tape**

## GETTING READY

**1** Slide a penny and dime through a gum wrapper to be sure they won't get stuck. If either of the coins gets stuck, open the wrapper and widen it a bit so the coins *can* slide through. Then fold one end over to close it off, and tape the wrapper to the bottom of a small paper plate, near one edge. The open end must be facing the edge of the plate.

**2** Slide the penny and dime into the wrapper and you are ready.

## SHOWTIME!

**1** Show three coins to your friends and place them onto the plate.

**2** Tell your friends, "This is my magic wish dish. Whenever I want more coins, I just put what I've got on the dish and I wish real hard. I'm going to wish for five this time."

**3** Tell one of your friends to open his hand. Tip the plate toward your friend's hand so that the two coins from underneath slide out to join the ones already on the plate, into his waiting hand! (The three coins on the plate will cover the two coming out from underneath.)

# THE LAZY
# MAGICIAN

*You choose a volunteer to perform your next trick. Your volunteer chooses a card and places it back into the deck, then makes it magically turn over with a wave of the hand!*

## WHAT YOU'LL NEED
• **deck of cards** • **table**

## GETTING READY

Turn over the bottom card of a deck and return it to the bottom with the back facing out. The deck now looks the same on the bottom and top.

## SHOWTIME!

❶ Ask someone to volunteer to perform this trick. Spread the cards out on the table so your volunteer can select one. Be careful as you spread them out that the bottom, reversed card is not seen.

❷ After your volunteer selects a card, close the deck so it sits in the palm of one hand. As your volunteer looks at the card she has selected, secretly turn the deck over so the reversed bottom card is now on top of the deck. When your volunteer looks back at you, it will appear as if nothing has happened.

❸ Take the card from your volunteer and, keeping the face of it away from you, bury it facedown in the middle of the deck. What you have actually done is placed the selected card *backward* in the deck of cards.

❹ Say to your volunteer, "You are going to do the magic here. Let me show you how." Turn the hand holding the deck palm down and place the deck on the table. The deck is now right-side up again, with the reversed card on the bottom. Only, *now* it also has the selected card reversed.

❻ Have your volunteer wave her hand over the deck. You then pick up the deck and spread through the cards from hand to hand until you reach one card, the selected one, reversed. Have your volunteer turn it around, then say, "Very good! Have you ever considered taking up magic as a hobby?"

# THE MORPHING STRINGS

*You magically morph two strings into one!*

## WHAT YOU'LL NEED

• piece of string about 24 inches long (must be made up of many thin strands)

## GETTING READY

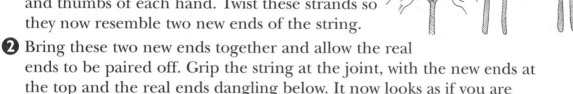

❶ Grip the string about halfway down, using your index fingers and thumbs, and pull, separating all the strands. You should be holding nearly equal amounts of strands between the index fingers and thumbs of each hand. Twist these strands so they now resemble two new ends of the string.

❷ Bring these two new ends together and allow the real ends to be paired off. Grip the string at the joint, with the new ends at the top and the real ends dangling below. It now looks as if you are holding two strings.

## SHOWTIME!

❶ Show the "two" strings in your fingers (your left if you're right-handed, right if you're left-handed).

❷ Close your other hand into a fist around the top ends and joint, letting go with your opposite fingers. Don't expose the joint while doing this!

❸ Ask your friend to hold one of the bottom ends. You hold the other bottom end with the hand that just let go of the top ends and joint.

❹ Instruct your friend to pull slowly on his or her end. You do the same. As the two of you pull, the string will slowly emerge from your fist back together as one string. The "two" strings have magically morphed into one!

# OUT OF
# THE BAG

*You reach into an "empty" bag with an empty hand and produce a ball!*

## WHAT YOU'LL NEED
• **folded-up paper lunch bag** • **small ball** • **secret helper**

## GETTING READY

**❶** Put the folded-up paper lunch bag into your pocket.

**❷** Give a small ball to your secret helper. He will be sitting in the audience with everyone else.

## SHOWTIME!

**❶** Remove the folded bag from your pocket and open it up. Say, "Here is an empty bag. You know it's completely empty because it was folded flat."

**❷** Walk over to someone in the audience and say, "Look inside. Is it empty?" The person will confirm that it is. Tell the person to feel around inside. "Do you feel anything?" Again the person will say it is empty.

**❸** Turn to another person and ask him or her to feel inside. This person will feel inside and say it is empty.

**❹** Now turn to your secret helper as if he is just another audience member and ask him to feel inside also.

**❺** When your secret helper reaches inside, he drops the ball he is secretly holding into the bag when he removes his hand. Your secret helper must then say that the bag is empty.

**❻** Face the entire audience and say, "Empty! No question about it. But *watch!*" Snap your fingers over the bag. Show that your hand is empty, and then reach into the bag and remove the ball.

# THE IMAGE
# OF YOUR CARD

*Here's a sneaky way to find out what card your friend has chosen!*

## WHAT YOU'LL NEED
**• boxed deck of cards • small mirror • glue • table**

## GETTING READY

❶ Glue a small mirror securely onto the back of a box of cards (it should not extend beyond the sides of the box). You may have to let this dry overnight.

❷ Have the deck of cards in the box, with the box flap closed, at the start of the trick.

## SHOWTIME!

❶ Holding the box of cards in one hand, with the mirror side facing toward you, remove the deck of cards with your other hand and spread the cards out on the table, facedown.

❷ Ask a volunteer to choose a card. Have this person look at the card and hand it to you to hold.

❸ You take the card with your free hand (remember, you are still holding the box with the mirror facing you) and hold it so the number and suit of the card faces your volunteer at all times. Position it behind the box so its reflection can be seen in the mirror.

❹ Tell your volunteer to concentrate. "Try to mentally send me the image of your card," you tell him. While you are saying this, get a quick glimpse of the card in the mirror. Say, "I believe I am getting an image of your card," then proudly announce the name of the selected card.

# A DELICATE
# BALANCE

*A simple and quick balancing trick that only you can perform!*

## WHAT YOU'LL NEED

• **three small drinking glasses, all the same size** • **table** • **a piece of construction paper**

## SHOWTIME!

❶ Set up two of the glasses on the table, about 6 inches apart, mouth down. Lay the paper across the glasses and challenge your friend to place the third glass in the center of the paper and make it balance there. Tell him or her to be careful to not break the glass. Your friend will try and fail.

❷ Once your friend gives up, pick up the paper and fold it accordion style. You can now lay it back across the two glasses and place the third in the center. The folds in the paper help to strengthen it so it will be able to support the weight of the glass.

# WHERE DID IT GO?

*After folding a coin up in a small square of paper, the coin vanishes!*

## WHAT YOU'LL NEED
• square piece of paper, approximately 4 by 4 inches • table • quarter

## SHOWTIME!

❶ Put the paper square on the table and place the quarter in the center.

❷ Fold the right side of the paper over the quarter so the right edge just passes the left side of the coin. Crease this fold.

❸ Fold the left side of the paper over the quarter so it slightly overlaps the close edge of the first folded piece. Crease this fold.

❹ Now pick up the paper and hold it vertically. Your fingers should be facing the audience and your thumb facing you. (The thumb holds the coin in place.) With your other hand, begin folding the top down, toward you. At the same time, the thumb holding the coin releases enough pressure to allow the coin to slide out the bottom of the paper into the palm of your hand.

❺ Once the top is folded down and creased, fold the bottom upward, toward you. Be careful not to expose the coin now hidden in your hand.

❻ Once the bottom is folded and creased, you will have a smaller folded square of paper. Put it on the table and step back. Call out a magic word or two, and have a volunteer open the paper. Use this opportunity to get rid of the coin hidden in your hand by secretly placing it in your pocket.

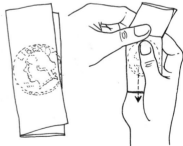

75

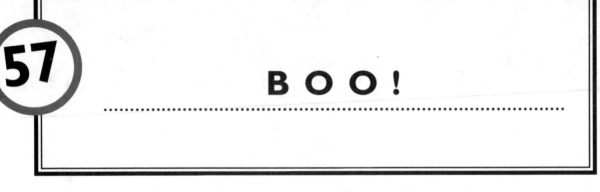

## 57

# B O O !

........................................................................................................

A *ghost magically appears on a blank card that was signed by your friend moments before.*

## WHAT YOU'LL NEED

• **black marker** • **stack of 3- by 5-inch index cards** • **rubber bands** • **table**

## GETTING READY

**❶** Cut an index card, 3 by 5 inches, in half. Discard one of the halves.

**❷** Take another 3- by 5-inch index card and on one half of it, use a black marker to draw a ghost or some other monster.

**❸** Cover this picture with the half card, and place this setup on top of a stack of index cards. Line the cards up so no part of the picture is seen sticking out from under the half card.

**❹** Wrap a few rubber bands around the center of the stack. The bands should hide the edge of the half card and keep it in place. You now have what looks like a stack of blank index cards. Grab your marker, and you are ready.

# SHOWTIME!

**❶** Give the marker to a friend and ask her to sign her name on the top card of the stack of index cards sitting on the table.

**❷** Push the stack of cards toward your friend, making sure that the end without the half card is nearest her. Point to that end of the card as you ask your friend to sign. She will think she is signing a blank card.

**❸** Once your friend has signed the card, pick up the whole stack by its sides and turn it facedown. Slide your thumb between the signed card and the rest of the stack and grip the card by the end that has been signed. Pull it out and, keeping it facedown, place it on the table.

**❹** Now tell your friend to write the word "GHOST" (or "MONSTER," depending on the picture you've drawn) on the back of the card.

**❺** Once this has been done, take the marker back and wave it over the card. Watch your friend's face when she turns the card over and sees the picture that has magically appeared!

# SEEIN' SPOTS!

Every time your friend stacks dice, you correctly guess the amount of hidden spots on them!

## WHAT YOU'LL NEED
• four dice

## SHOWTIME!

❶ Ask a volunteer to stack the dice any way he chooses while your back is turned.

❷ Once this has been done, you turn back around and announce that you will attempt to guess the total sum of all the spots you can't see.

❸ Hold your hand over the stack for a few moments, as if in concentration. What you are really doing is some quick math. If you look at a single die and total the top and bottom numbers together, they will *always* equal 7. There are 4 dice being used in this trick. Therefore, 4 x 7 = 28. All you need to do as you hold your hand over the stack is look at the top number on the stack and subtract it from 28. *That* is the number you call out to your volunteer.

❹ Once you announce your guess, allow your volunteer to disassemble the dice, totaling the numbers as he goes. You will be correct every time!

# THE SPOOKY SINGING GOBLET

*You and your friends, seated around a table with a goblet of water in the center, join hands. No one, you say, is allowed to break the chain. The lights are turned off, and everyone concentrates. Soon eerie music begins to come from the goblet!*

## WHAT YOU'LL NEED
• table • secret helper • goblet of water, three-fourths full

## SHOWTIME!

**1** Gather your friends around the table. Your secret helper must sit in the chair to your right. Place the goblet of water in the middle of the table.

**2** Instruct everyone to join hands, and make it clear you do not want the chain broken. Have someone turn out the lights. In the darkness, speak softly and tell everyone to picture the goblet in their minds and to concentrate.

**3** While this is being done, you let go with the hand your secret helper is holding and silently dip your index finger into the water. Now, by rubbing your wet finger around the lip of the glass, you will create a ringing tone that sounds very spooky . . . especially in the dark.

**4** Only do this for a few moments, and then stop. Quickly grab your secret helper's hand again and call for the lights to be turned on. When they come on, all will look normal.

---

**NOTE:** Not *all* goblets will work for this trick. Be sure you try a few out beforehand to discover which one produces the best ringing sound.

# THE RISING
# CARD

*...d you name rises out of the deck.*

## WHAT YOU'LL NEED
• deck of cards

## SHOWTIME!

❶ Have the deck shuffled by a volunteer.

❷ Once the deck is given back to you, quickly note which card is on top as you straighten the deck. Let's say it is the 2 of clubs.

❸ Hold the deck vertically in your palm (your left if you're right-handed, right if you're left-handed) so the number on the bottom card faces the audience.

❹ Extend the index finger of your other hand and, with it, touch the top end of the deck. Once your finger is in contact with the deck, secretly extend your little finger and touch it to the back of the top card.

❺ Now call out, "Two of clubs . . . rise!" At that moment, push upward on the top card with your little finger. Do this slowly. From the audience's viewpoint, all that's seen is your index finger extended above a rising card. It will appear to the audience that the card is rising from the middle of the deck!